2/05   8.50

The
Box Turtle
Manual

DISCARD

PHILIPPE DE VOSJOLI   ROGER KLINGENBERG, D.V.M.

Table of Contents

Acknowledgements

The author wishes to thank Roger Klingenberg for coming to the rescue to improve the material on the recognition and treatment of diseases and Bill Love of Glades Herp for coming through with great color photographs.

INTRODUCTION

Box turtles aren't Mutant Ninja Turtles and they don't particularly care for pizza.

Although box turtles rank among the most popular and beautiful of all turtles (virtually no other turtle can match an outstanding male eastern box turtle), they are also among the most neglected and mistreated of all turtles sold in pet stores. Unwillingness to confront the health problems common to commercially collected box turtles, and the lack of

Male eastern box turtle *(Terrapene carolina carolina)*.

readily available information on their requirements are the primary reasons for the failure of these turtles to establish in captivity.

This book was written for people who care about box turtles and who appreciate their beauty and interesting behavior. If you think of a box turtle as merely an inexpensive and relatively disposable child's pet, save yourself some money—and save a box turtle—by simply not acquiring one. Remember, box turtles are not Mutant Ninja Turtles. They can't live in damp, dark sewage systems. On the other hand, box turtles have been on earth thousands of years longer than any mutant turtles. They may teach you one or two lessons about the delicate balance of life, natural law, and the many ways in which intelligence is manifested in nature.

The purpose of this book is to present background information and guidelines for care that we hope will lead to increased survival of these turtles in the pet trade and in the homes of prospective owners. A section is included on the care of two species of Asian box turtles of the genus *Cuora*, which are now commonly sold in the pet trade.

General Care and Maintenance of Box Turtles

Philippe de Vosjoli

Box turtles are beautiful. They are interesting. But they are also inexpensive, and at times overexploited, neglected, and miscared for. In fact, the majority of animals collected for the pet trade die within the first year in captivity.

Yet several books on amphibians and reptiles consistently rank box turtles as relatively easy to care for and as ideal pet turtles. This information will contradict the experience of many first-time turtle owners who have had problems and more problems (sometimes ending in death) with box turtles.

Why this contradiction? Didn't the writers of those books know what they were talking about? The fact is that the information on the care of box turtles in many herpetological books conveyed a different perspective from the one we experience today. At one time there was none of the large-scale commercial collecting and marketing of box turtles that has emerged over the last twenty years. In the past, most box turtles were collected and kept locally by individuals and their families or brought to the local pet store. As a result, box turtles were commonly kept relatively isolated and under climatic conditions to which they were

Because of the way American box turtles are maintained following collection in the wild, a relatively high percentage of turtles sold in the pet stores will become sick and require treatment.

more or less adapted. Today, box turtles are collected by the hundreds and thousands by commercial collectors in the states where they still can be legally collected and where they still exist in substantial numbers. Depending on the collecting methods, these turtles may be stuffed into burlap bags or piled into boxes. They are later released into holding compounds, where they are usually kept in overcrowded conditions.

Depending on how these turtles are maintained in these holding compounds, they may contract diseases spread through vectors such as water and food. If the animals are kept too cool, they may develop respiratory disorders. Parasite and bacterial infections also tend to spread among the group. At some point, box turtles are shipped to pet distributors who may continue to maintain them under varying degrees of overcrowding, although increasing numbers of specialized reptile wholesalers are now making

If you are buying a box turtle for your children, please keep in mind that children are incapable of providing adequate care for a box turtle without supervision by a responsible adult. Box turtles are not children's playthings.

concerted efforts to provide improved conditions for maintaining these animals. The turtles are then shipped and delivered to retail outlets. The end result is that the box turtles sold in pet stores are not the same "hardy" box turtles that are mentioned in various books. Many are stressed, diseased, and dehydrated. In fact, reptile distributors often speak of good versus bad groups of collected box turtles, depending on their overall state of health or their rate of mortality. Thus, it is possible to successfully establish box turtles sold in the pet trade only if one acknowledges the problems associated with collected animals and contends with their condition.

Before Buying a Box Turtle

In order to fare well in capitivity, box turtles require more care than many other turtle species sold in pet stores. Box turtles are special animals; you should not let their low purchase price give you the illusion that they are expendable animals. The day that the only box turtles available are captive-bred and -raised animals, you will realize that an adult box turtle is worth considerably more than you have paid for it—when you consider the time, labor, and cost of raising it to adulthood. For herpetoculturists in other countries, American box turtles are considered to be special prizes, among the most desirable of turtles.

The Future of Box Turtles

If no efforts are made to manage wild box turltes and to establish captive breeding programs, before very long they will all be protected and unavailable. Herpetoculturists should strive to change current United States laws that restrict the commercial sales of turtles under four inches so that captive breeding of box turtles becomes practical. In addition, laws should be passed to make the sales of turtles to minors illegal. All sales should require a release form whereby adults acknowledge and accept the risks involved, including salmonellosis. Every retailer would be expected to provide information on hygiene practices to reduce the risks of contracting salmonellosis.

Basic Hygiene for Box Turtle Owners

◆ Keep the captive environment of turtles clean. Regularly change water and disinfect water dish with a five-percent bleach solution; rinse well before refilling.

◆ Always wash hands after handling any turtle, preferably using Betadine® scrub or an anti-bacterial soap.

◆ Do not allow children to handle turtles without parental or adult supervision. Inform children that they should not put their fingers in their mouth when handling a turtle. Also, they should not kiss any turtle.

◆ Do not allow turtles loose in the home unless they have been checked for salmonella. Generally allowing turtles loose in a home is not a good idea.

◆ Never wash a turtle enclosure and/or associated materials, or allow turtles to soak in any sink or tub or dishpan used by or for humans. If there are no alternatives, disinfect afterward with a five-percent bleach solution. Always wash hands after maintaining turtle enclosures.

GENERAL INFORMATION

North American box turtles comprise four species in the large turtle family Emydidae. The following box turtles are currently offered in pet stores:

♦ The eastern box turtle *(Terrapene carolina carolina)*

♦ The three-toed box turtle *(Terrapene carolina triunguis)*

♦ The Gulf Coast box turtle *(Terrapene carolina major)*

♦ The ornate box turtle *(Terrapene ornata)*

All of the subspecies of *Terrapene carolina* may intergrade with others in parts of their range.

The common name "box turtle" was given to these turtles and others because of their ability to withdraw their heads and limbs within their shells and effectively seal themselves in (as if in a box), thanks to a plastral hinge that allows for movement of sections of the plastron (the lower part of the shell).

Distribution

American box turtles come from the eastern, central, and southwestern United States and from Mexico.

An Overview of American Box Turtles

Terrapene carolina carolina (Linnaeus 1758), Eastern box turtle, NE United States (Maine to Georgia, westwards to Michigan, Illinois, Tennessee)

Terrapene carolina bauri (Taylor 1895), Florida box turtle, SE United States (Florida)

Terrapene carolina major (Agassiz 1857), Gulf Coast box turtle, SE United States (Gulf Coast from W Florida to Texas)

Terrapene carolina mexicana (Gray 1849), Mexican box turtle, E Mexico (Nuevo Leon southwards to Vera Cruz)

Terrapene carolina triunguis (Agassiz 1857), Three-toed box turtle, Central and S United States (from Missouri southwards to Texas and Alabama)

Terrapene carolina yucatana (Boulenger 1895), Yucatan box turtle, SE Mexico (Yucatan and Quintana Roo)

Terrapene coahuila (Schmidt and Owens 1944), Coahuila box turtle, NE Mexico (Coahuila)

Terrapene nelsoni nelsoni (Stejneger 1925), Nayarit box turtle, NE Mexico (Nayarit)

Terrapene nelsoni klauberi (Bogert 1943), Klauber's box turtle, NW Mexico (S Sonora)

Terrapene ornata ornata (Agassiz 1857), Ornate box turtle, Central and S United States (from S Dakota and Illinois southwards to Arizona and Texas)

Terrapene ornata luteola (Smith and Ransay 1952), Desert box turtle, S United States (S Texas) and NE Mexico (Coahuila to Tamaulipas)

Protection

Certain species and/or subspecies of box turtles are protected in several states, including Florida, Maine, Michigan, New Jersey, New York, and Virginia. Check with your local fish and game agencies for state regulations regarding the collection and possession of reptiles.

Size

The following are average adult sizes for the various box turtles offered in the pet trade.

+ Eastern box turtle: $4^1/_2$ to 6 inches; record size, $7^{13}/_{16}$ inches

+ Three-toed box turtle: $4^1/_2$ to 5 inches; record size, $6^1/_2$ inches

+ Gulf coast box turtle 5 to 7 inches; record size, $8^1/_2$ inches

+ Ornate box turtle: 4 to 5 inches; record size, $5^3/_4$ inches

Females are generally smaller than males. Hatchling box turtles average $1^1/_8$ inches to $1^1/_4$ inches.

Growth

Hatchlings will grow to an adult size of four to five inches in four to six years, depending on the conditions under which they are raised. Their diet, their temperature, and whether or not they are hibernated will determine their growth rate. Turtles that are not hibernated and are fed year round until their fourth year will grow at a significantly greater rate than turtles raised under natural conditions—that is, allowed to hibernate and be off feed for several months out of the year.

Captive-raised males can reach sexual maturity at four years. Females seldom breed successfully until they are at least five years of age, possibly six or seven years. Once the four- to five-inch length is achieved, growth slows down considerably. Animals more than ten years old demonstrate little annual shell growth.

Terminology

The following are some basic terms you will need to know when referring to parts of a turtle.

- ◆ Carapace: The upper part of the shell of a turtle

- ◆ Plastron: The lower part of the shell of a turtle

- ◆ Scutes: The horny plates that make up the surface of a turtle's shell

Sexing

Box turtles are easily sexed reptiles. As a rule, male box turtles grow larger than females. The males of some subspecies, particularly eastern box turtles, are also markedly more colorful than females. Many males of this subspecies have brightly colored heads and limbs, and their eyes bear orange-yellow irises. In the *Terrapene carolina* complex (the eastern, Gulf Coast, and three-toed box turtles), the most obvious features of males are the concave posterior lobe of the plastron and longer tail, versus the flat plastron and the shorter tail of females. Other charateristics that allow for sexing include the base of the tail, which is thicker in males than in females, and the greater distance of the vent (the opening to the cloaca) from the body in males when the tail is extended.

In ornate box turtles *(Terrapene ornata)*, sexing is best done by checking for longer and thicker tails in males. In this species there is no plastral concavity in males; the plastron will appear to be flat in both sexes.

Gulf coast box turtles *(Terrapene carolina major).* Female on left and male on right. Note the plastral concavity of the male.

Note the differences in tail lengths between female (left) and male (right) box turtles. In males, the base of the tail is also thicker.

Longevity

Slavens (1992) mentions record lifespans in captivity of 22 years 7 months for the Florida box turtle *(Terrapene carolina bauri)*, 26 years 5 months for the eastern box turtle *(Terrapene carolina carolina)*, and 26 years 5 months for the three-toed box turtle *(Terrapene carolina triunguis)*. It is worth noting that both record life spans in Slavens (1992) for the ornate box turtle *(Terrapene ornata)* are less than seven years. From a hatchling, the potential lifespan of a box turtle is considered to be 30 to 40 years, but many specimens live considerably longer. There are a few reports of individuals estimated to be more than 100 years old.

SELECTING A POTENTIALLY HEALTHY BOX TURTLE

Selecting what appears to be a healthy box turtle will be critical to your long-term success with this species. The following are guidelines that can help you select a potentially healthy box turtle.

1. Select a turtle that appears alert and active. When possible, choose the smallest, and therefore the youngest, in a group. Smaller animals typically adapt better to captivity.

2. Pick up the turtle. The turtle should feel as if it has some weight to it; it should not feel as if you are picking up a

Male three-toed box turtle *(Terrapene carolina triunguis)*. This alert and healthy appearing animal would be a good choice for a pet box turtle.

nearly empty shell. Pick up a few other turtles as well, in order to get a sense of differences in weight.

3. Now inspect the turtle carefully. Look at the top part of the shell and examine it for any damage. Look at the bottom part of the shell and check for any signs of shell damage or of hemorrhage beneath or between the scutes (the individual scales of the shell). Avoid turtles with any such symptoms. Bleeding underneath the scutes can be a sign of septicemia, which will be fatal if it is left untreated. [See Diseases and Disorders.]

4. Now examine the limbs. Look for signs of swelling. Avoid turtles with swollen limbs or any signs of infection. Gently pull on a hind leg. A healthy turtle will have a strong withdrawal response and try to pull that leg in. There should be a definite feeling of vigor when you pull on the leg. Avoid turtles that don't have strong pull and that don't demonstrate a certain amount of muscle tone and vigor.

5. Look carefully at the head. Avoid turtles with swollen eyelids and/or closed eyes. Look for signs of swelling on the sides of the head. Avoid turtles that have one or both "cheeks" swollen.

6. Now look for signs of a respiratory infection. Examine the nostrils and look for signs of bubbly mucus. Avoid turtles with bubbly mucus. If the turtle has its head out, gently press up against its throat with your thumb; if mucus emerges from the nostrils, this is a sign of a respiratory infection. Avoid turtles with this symptom. Check for puffing out of the throat or extending of the neck, followed by gaping of the mouth. These are also symptoms of respiratory infection.

7. Gently tap on the turtle's head to see what kind of withdrawal response you get. Healthy box turtles have a strong withdrawal response.

8. Examine the tail area. Check for any signs of infection, swelling, diarrhea, or prolapse (protrusion of cloaca or intestine through the vent). Avoid turtles with any of these symptoms.

Box turtles display a variety of social behavior that makes their keeping in groups even more enjoyable than keeping them singly.

Keeping Box Turtles in Groups

Several male and female box turtles can be kept together in large enclosures. In captivity the success rate of breeding is known to increase when several members of both sexes are kept together.

Acclimation

There are several problems that are commonly encountered with box turtles purchased in pet stores. Many of these problems can be avoided by following the previously mentioned steps. Some of the more common problems encountered in collected box turtles are:

♦ Reluctance to feed

♦ Respiratory disorders

♦ Parasites

♦ Abscesses.

Any newly purchased box turtle will require a period of acclimation, so that the turtle can adjust to captive conditions. Steps to assist the animal's acclimation can be summarized as follows:

1. Place the turtle in a suitable enclosure with adequate heat.

2. Offer clean water at all times in a shallow dish.

3. Provide a shelter or a medium for burrowing.

4. Offer food every other day.

5. If the turtle has a respiratory disorder provide additional heat. If the respiratory problem is severe, have it treated with antibiotics [see Diseases and Disorders].

6. Treat the turtle routinely for nematode parasites [see Diseases and Disorders].

7. Treat the turtle for protozoan parasites [see Diseases and Disorders].

8. Treat other initial problems as they occur during the acclimation period.

HOUSING AND MAINTENANCE

There are two approaches to keeping box turtles, depending on where you are living: they can be kept outdoors or they can be kept indoors. Commonly the best solution is a combination of both, keeping them outdoors part of the year and indoors at other times of the year.

Outdoor Enclosures

Whenever possible you should keep box turtles in large outdoor vivaria, which can be designed to provide conditions that meet their needs. As a rule, *Terrapene carolina* require moderately warm daytime temperatures (70 to 85° F or 21.1 to 29.4° C) and tolerate nighttime temperatures in the 50s° F (10 to 15° C) during spring, summer, and fall. One criterion for keeping this species outdoors should be the relative humidity. *Terrapene carolina* requires a medium to high relative humidity for outdoor keeping; it is not a suitable species for keeping outdoors in desert areas of the United States.

The ornate box turtle is a dweller of the prairies and is better suited for keeping in dry, warm areas, but you must provide it with a burrow or shelter with high humidity. In the wild, this species spends most of its time in burrows where relative humidity is considerably higher than it is at the ground surface.

Box turtles in a simple outdoor setup.

There are no simple answers to the design of outdoor vivaria. If you are willing to spend the money, you can design outdoor enclosures to provide the proper conditions for almost any species. A section covered with greenhouse-style clear fiberglass roofing, for example, can provide additional heat through a greenhouse effect, as well as higher humidity if the inside is regularly misted or sprayed with water. Some people provide additional heat by creating shelters warmed by an incandescent spotlight. They may also create insulated subterranean shelters to provide a cool section during the summer heat. Other herpetoculturists install heating systems. Many create indoor/outdoor environments that together provide optimal conditions for the maintenance of a particular species of turtle.

Basic Outdoor Setup

For outdoor setups, the minimum enclosure size should measure four feet by two feet for two animals, preferably larger for more animals. The outdoor enclosure should be located in a yard in such a way that it is always partially shaded but also receives sunlight for part of the day. If a shaded area is not available, you should create one. Plant some shrubs in one section of the enclosure to provide shade and shelter. Also include a shelter made out of wood to provide shelter from the elements. Hollowed wood logs or stumps and large rounded cork bark sections make ideal and natural-looking shelters for box turtle vivaria. Also set aside an area for sinking a shallow water pan or for custom designing a shallow concrete pool.

You can construct an outdoor box turtle vivarium of either wood or concrete blocks. In both cases, the walls of the vivarium should extend into the ground eight to twelve inches, thus creating a barrier that will prevent turtles from digging out of the enclosure. Some turtle keepers build walls of wood frame with welded wire above an underground barrier of poured concrete.

Screen Tops

You should build a screen top for outdoor enclosures and install it on top of the enclosure; this will serve to keep away unwanted animals. In areas that receive too much sunlight, you can use shade cloth as a screen material.

Indoor Setups

Many people keep their box turtles indoors, either because they live in apartments or because other living conditions, such as harsh outdoor weather, make indoor vivaria the best option for keeping these turtles.

Aquarium tanks, 30 gallons or more, are suitable for keeping box turtles, but indoor enclosures can easily be built of wood.

The minimum size of enclosure for a single box turtle should be at least 36 inches long and at least 12 inches wide; larger is better. For keeping two to three box turtles, enclosures at least 48 inches long are recommended. The height should be at least 15 inches. The inside of wood enclosures should be coated with one or two coats of epoxy paint to make the wood waterproof. Some people use two or three coats of polyurethane (a product with a nontoxic solvent base) for this purpose. Commercially sold containers that

A concrete mixing container designed as a box turtle enclosure.

work well with box turtles are large plastic concrete-mixing containers available in hardware stores.

Ground Medium

A two- to three-inch layer of a high-quality, slightly moistened, peat-based potting soil (without perlite) mixed with a fine grade of orchid bark can be used as a ground medium for a box turtle vivarium. Ideally you should provide a medium that allows for burrowing, that can hold moisture to increase relative humidity, and which has a surface which will dry rapidly.

Another medium that has been used with success is a medium grade of fir or orchid bark.

You can use other materials, as long as you are careful to avoid soggy media and coarse media such as silica sand or coarse aquarium gravel, which can abrade the shell and can lead to shell infections.

If you use newspaper or brown paper to allow for easy cleaning, then you should include a container with potting soil under a shelter, in order to provide a medium for burrowing and an area of high relative humidity.

Landscaping

The only other essential landscaping feature in the turtle vivarium is a shelter. This is best built out of wood. It should be of a height approximately one inch greater than the height of the shell of your box turtles when they are standing. As an alternative, large sections of rounded cork bark (available from specialized reptile dealers) are ideal shelters for box turtles.

Heating

Heating in the vivarium is crucial to acclimating newly purchased box turtles and is essential for their long-term survival in captivity. A significant percentage of box turtles purchased by the general public die because of inadequate heating. Many of the problems initially encountered with newly purchased box turtles can be remedied with adequate heat.

Indoor box turtle enclosures can be heated using both of the following methods.

♦ An area with a heated floor. If you choose to use an aquarium tank, you can purchase some of the subtank heating units for reptiles currently available in pet stores. Alternatively, you can buy a large "hot rock"-type heater and bury it in the ground medium. Some people put an inverted aluminum pan over a hot rock to diffuse the heat.

At least fifty percent of a vivarium should be unheated so that box turtles can thermoregulate. Overheated vivaria can cause distress, weaken the immune system, and even kill box turtles.

♦ An overhead heat source. In addition to a ground-level heat source, you should place at one end of the vivarium an incandescent light or spotlight over a basking area, so that heat at the area nearest the bulb measures 84 to 88° F (28.8 to 31.1° C). This light should be set on a timer to be on twelve to fourteen hours each day during spring, summer, and fall.

Other Lighting

For indoor keeping, giving your pet daily exposure to full-spectrum fluorescent lights has psychological benefits. These lights are recommended but not required for the successful maintenance of box turtles. You must place the lights within two feet of the turtles themselves, in order to produce these beneficial effects.

Relative Humidity

Relative humidity is a critical factor in the successful keeping of box turtles. The relative humidity should be 60 to 80 percent for the *Terrapene carolina* complex. Under low relative humidity conditions, many box turtles burrow if given the opportunity. In captivity, box turtles may become stressed if they are unable to burrow when kept at a low relative humidity; they also may develop eye and ear infections under these conditions. When you keep box turtles indoors, one method of dealing with low relative humidity is to keep them on a layer of medium-grade pea gravel. By adding water to a depth of one-third to one-half that of the pea gravel layer, the relative humidity is raised as a result of water evaporation from the substrate. Daily misting also helps. Outdoors, you can increase relative humidity by providing shrubs for shade and shelter and by misting the enclosure each day. Placing a misting system on a timer is a labor-saving way of providing moisture to outdoor enclosures.

Dogs and Box Turtles

Dogs frequently find box turtles to be an appealing kind of crunchy sushi. Box turtles, whether kept outside or inside, must be protected from predation by dogs. Typically, dogs chew off pieces from the edge of the turtle's shell. Large dogs may succeed in cracking the shell and can then kill the turtle. To prevent such disasters, cover your setups with a wood frame and wire mesh top if your turtles are likely to be exposed to dogs.

Raccoons and opossums also find most turtles to be tasty tidbits.

Courtesy of Reptile Haven.

Basic indoor setup for a pair of box turtles. Artificial grass is a suitable medium for members of the *Terrapene carolina* complex but a burrowing medium should be provided for ornate box turtles.

Box turtles kept outdoors frequently dig shelters under landscape structures.

FEEDING BOX TURTLES

There are many books on the market that convey the wrong information on the diet of box turtles. The following are proven guidelines for feeding box turtles. In a broad sense, box turtles are opportunistic omnivores, which accounts for their relatively high densities (until recently) in many areas of the United States. The hatchlings and juveniles are primarily carnivorous; as they grow older they gradually consume more plant material.

Many of the wild-collected animals sold in pet shops may be reluctant feeders at first. The key to establishing a healthy feeding routine in box turtles is to set up daily patterns that will stimulate and lead to regular and eager feeding.

When to Feed

If box turtles are kept outdoors, wait until the morning temperatures have started to warm up before you offer food.

Box turtles must be allowed to warm up before they are fed. Make sure that the heating units in your indoor vivarium have been turned on for a couple of hours before offering food to your turtle. When they are not hibernating, box turtles of all ages should be offered food every other day.

What to Feed

Box turtles recognize food by sight and by smell. To entice box turtles to feed, you must stimulate both these senses.

Box turtles should be offered food in two categories at each feeding: (1) meat products or live foods and (2) plant matter.

Meat Products

♦ Low-fat canned dog food (You may have to experiment with these; foods containing chicken are typically relished by these turtles.)

♦ Finely cut cooked chicken

♦ Finely cut pieces of beef heart

Live Foods

The movement displayed by live foods usually draws the attention of box turtles. Sometimes live foods can be the key to persuading a box turtle to feed. Offering live prey to box turtles will also reveal interesting reactions and an amusing side to the box turtle's character. Few turtles display as much expression as a box turtle eyeing a prey item and, with the determination and vigor so characteristic of turtles, chasing down that prey to catch and eat it. You should offer live foods on a regular basis as an essential part of a box turtle's diet. All live prey must be offered in low feeding dishes to prevent them from escaping and burrowing into the ground medium.

The following are recommended live foods.

1. Live crickets. Keep live crickets in a small plastic terrarium overnight and offer them nutritious foods before feeding them to turtles. Give the crickets tropical fish flakes or finely ground rodent or monkey chow, along with a slice of orange and/or grated carrots. Try to pinch off the hind legs before offering. This is a simple procedure: pick up a cricket, hold it between the thumb and index finger, and pinch the hind legs at the level of the "knee" joints. This procedure will cause crickets to "drop" their hind legs, thereby enabling box turtles to catch the crickets more easily.

As a rule, the best approach to feeding box turtles is to offer a varied diet.

2. Mealworms *(Tenebrio)* and king mealworms *(Zoophobas).* These worms should also be given a high quality diet before you offer them to the turtle. Offer small numbers per feeding (one to three king mealworms per adult animal or three to five regular mealworms), as your turtle may regurgitate them if it eats too many at once. The chitinous, nondigestible exoskeleton of these insects can make them difficult to digest if they are not well "chewed" or if too many are eaten. You can raise your own mealworms and offer soft, just molted, or "white" mealworms and king mealworms, which are more easily digested.

3. Earthworms. Garden worms, bait store worms, and small nightcrawlers will be relished by box turtles if they are offered in moderate amounts. Offering live earthworms is a good way to get reluctant box turtles to feed.

4. Pink mice. Small, one- to two-day-old "pink" mice make a good food for box turtles. After a few feedings, box turtles readily feed on pre-killed "pinkies." Dip the rumps of the pink mice in a reptile vitamin/mineral powder prior t o feeding, because newborn mice can be calcium deficient.

5. Other live foods. In addition to the previous suggestions, box turtles will readily feed on small slugs and snails, as well as on various insects, especially larvae. Just remember that variety is important in a well-balanced box turtle's diet.

Plant Matter

In addition to live foods, box turtles should be offered a variety of plant matter. It is essential for supplying adequate vitamins and nutrients for the maintenance of adult animals.

The following are some recommended plant foods.

1. Berries and red fruit: Colorful berries and fruit are always appealing to box turtles. They relish strawberries, raspberries, cranberries and blackberries. Other red fruits, such as cherries and plums, will also be eaten readily.

2. Other fruits: Box turtles should occasionally be offered small quantities of diced cantaloupe, banana, peach, apricot, and apple.

3. Vegetables and other greens: You also should offer box turtles various vegetables and greens on a regular basis. Good choices are thawed frozen mixed vegetables, romaine lettuce, green peppers, tomatoes, broccoli heads, cauliflower, and cooked sweet and regular potatoes.

Do not feed them pale lettuces such as iceberg, which have a very low nutritional value.

Other Foods

Some box turtles will take soaked ZU-Preem® monkey chow. This is a good food source when combined with fruits and other plant matter. Some box turtles will also feed on soaked dry dog food. Make sure to select a high-quality dog food that is low in fat.

Monkey chow or dog food should only make up a small part (up to twenty percent) of a varied diet.

˙Variety Is Important

A box turtle may eagerly feed for weeks on strawberries, cantaloupe, and dog food, and then suddenly become reluctant to feed on them. Simply offering some new food items will whet its appetite and it will begin to feed again. The fact is that box turtles in the wild take advantage of seasonal flushes of plant and animal matter. Their wild diet thus tends to be varied. In captivity, box turtles may become bored with a routine diet and have to be stimulated with some new juicy little tidbits.

If a box turtle refuses to feed in spite of the variety of foods you have offered, it is possible that it may be entering a fasting period. Box turtles in the wild (for example, many ornate box turtles) may fast during parts of the summer when the weather is unusually warm. Thus, a captive box turtle following its internal time schedule may decide to fast. As long as your turtle has adequate weight and is provided with proper environmental conditions, no harm should come to it during a fasting period of a few weeks.

Simply continue to offer a variety of food on a regular basis, and the turtle will eventually resume feeding.

On a daily basis during hot, dry weather, turning on a sprinkler over an outdoor enclosure for short periods of time may stimulate feeding. In indoor vivaria, daily misting with a hand sprayer will accomplish the same result.

Vitamin/Mineral Supplementation

Box turtles that are fed an adequate diet require minimal supplementation. Unfortunately, it is not always possible to carefully monitor the calcium, vitamin, and mineral intake of these animals. As a backup to assure adequate nutrient intake, offer a high-quality powdered reptile vitamin/mineral supplement, mixed in food and offered once every other day for feeding small animals and twice a week for older animals. Live foods such as crickets and mealworms should be coated with a supplement before feeding. Simply put them in a bag with some vitamin/mineral supplement and shake. Do not neglect this aspect of feeding your box turtles. Calcium deficiency is a common cause of death and deformity in many captive turtles, particularly among hatchlings and young animals.

In due time, even box turtles kept outdoors lose their fear and come toward their owners when it's feeding time.

A group of box turtles kept outdoors gathering for early morning feeding. Photo by Bill Love, courtesy of Glades Herp.

Color Fading and Diet

Many wild-collected box turtles lose a great deal of their bright coloration within their first year in captivity. This fading can be partially attributed to a diet lacking in certain plant pigments. It is important to feed your box turtle a varied diet with plant matter rich in yellow and red plant pigments. Supplementing the diet with small amounts of beta-carotene can be helpful in maintaining red coloration.

Water

Water is best provided in a large, shallow water pan that the turtles can readily get in and out of. The pan should be large enough for the turtle to sit in, with the depth of the water no more than one-third the height of the turtle's body. Change the water regularly and whenever it is soiled. Keep the pan clean and disinfected on a regular basis with a five-percent bleach solution. Newly acquired box turtles should be placed for 15 minutes in a pan with $^1/_4$ - $^1/_2$ inch of water on a daily basis for at least a week so that they may rehydrate.

Box turtles should have water available to them at all times.

A male eastern box turtle (*Terrapene carolina carolina*). Males of this subspecies rank among the most beautiful of the turtles. Efforts, including captive breeding, are urgently needed to manage this subspecies. *Photo by William B. Love, courtesy of Glades Herp.*

A female eastern box turtle. Hibernation/brumation is required for this subspecies to do well in captivity. It fares best in areas where it can be kept outdoors. *Photo by William B. Love, courtesy of Glades Herp.*

An intergrade box turtle *(Terrapene c. carolina x Terrapene c. major)* from Altha, Florida. *Photo by William B. Love, courtesy of Glades Herp.*

Pinky, an albino eastern box turtle captive-raised by Chris Estep. This turtle was raised indoors from a hatchling and is allowed a two to three month period of hibernation during the winter. As a rule captive-raised box turtles fare better in indoor vivaria than wild-caught animals. *Photo by Chris Estep.*

Gulf Coast box turtle *(Terrapene carolina major)*. This is the largest of the box turtles and the first to become available in the pet trade following a winter rest. This subspecies is often heavily parasitized, notably by botfly larvae. *Photo by William B. Love, courtesy of Glades Herp.*

Gulf Coast box turtle. White-headed specimens are common in some areas. *Photo by William B. Love, courtesy of Glades Herp*

A male western box turtle *(Terrapene ornata ornata)*. The green head is a characteristic of this sex. As a rule western box turtles fare poorly in captivity and are not recommended unless they can be kept outdoors in suitable climate and habitat. *Photo by William B. Love, courtesy of Glades Herp.*

A three-toed box turtle *(Terrapene c. triunguis)* clearly showing the attractive coloration of this subspecies. This is the most readily available box turtle in the pet trade; it is also the most adaptable. However, if efforts for management are not implemented and captive breeding programs are not developed, this species will eventually be protected. *Photo by William B. Love, courtesy of Glades Herp.*

A desert box turtle *(Terrapene ornata luteola)*. Photo by William B. Love, courtesy of Glades Herp.

A Mexican box turtle *(Terrapene carolina mexicana)*. This subspecies is not available in the reptile trade. Photo by William B. Love, courtesy of Glades Herp.

A Florida box turtle *(Terrapene carolina bauri)*. This attractive subspecies is protected in Florida and captive-bred specimens are rarely available in the reptile trade. *Photo by William B. Love, courtesy of Glades Herp.*

A Florida box turtle hatching. *Photo by William B. Love, courtesy of Glades Herp.*

The Coahuila *(Terrapene coahuila)* box turtle has remained aquatic and must be kept differently than other box turtles. It is not available in the general pet trade. *Photo by William B. Love, courtesy of Glades Herp.*

An Amboina or Malayan box turtle *(Cuora amboinensis)*. This Asian species is more aquatic than most North American box turtles. A sizeable water section should be included in their vivaria. Photo by John Tashjian, courtesy of Fort Worth Zoo.

A Chinese box turtle *(Cuora flavomarginata)*. This is an attractive and responsive species that tends to fare well in captivity when kept under the proper conditions. Photo by William B. Love, courtesy of Glades Herp.

An intergrade box turtle showing fire damage on the carapace. *Photo by William B. Love, courtesy of Glades Herp.*

Misting

Daily misting of box turtles is beneficial because it raises air humidity. It also can help stimulate a turtle's feeding.

Handling and Interaction

Box turtles are not really pets to be handled; they are best regarded as display animals with which some interaction may become possible. In time, box turtles learn to come to a food dish when food is offered. They may even become fearless enough to feed from their owner's hand. Individuals may also display various signs of intelligence, and some may follow their owners when they are hungry. Some turtles will come and stand on their owner's shoe or display other signs of association when they are hungry.

As with many other animals, the amount of time and attention you invest in your box turtle(s) will determine the type of relationship you will develop.

BREEDING BOX TURTLES

When they are maintained properly, box turtles will readily breed in captivity. The key to successful breeding is to have one or more healthy sexual pairs of animals and to provide a three-month hibernation period during the winter months.

Cooling/Hibernation

During the winter, healthy adult box turtles should be hibernated for three months where the air temperature can be maintained between 36 and 50° F (between 2.2 and 10° C). In many parts of the United States, a garage or unheated basement can be suitable for this purpose. In areas where winter temperatures seldom drop below 26° F (-3.3° C), box turtles can be kept outdoors year round and allowed to burrow in their pens. A bale of hay, partially spread out in one section of the outdoor enclosure, will provide additional burrowing material and insulation, which will allow box turtles more readily to tolerate cold outdoor temperatures.

To hibernate box turtles indoors, place them in a large container with as much as one foot of a loose and slightly moist peat-based potting soil. Over one-half of the soil surface, spread out a three-inch layer of loose hay. Cover the top of the container with a solid lid—such as a board in which several holes have been drilled—for air exchange. This lid will prevent the ground medium from drying out and will help maintain an adequate relative humidity level within the container. Box turtles will remain buried in the ground medium during the hibernation period as long as the temperatures remain low. Offer no food during the hibernation period, but keep a pan of water on the surface of the ground medium at all times.

You should check the container regularly during the hibernation period to make sure that the turtles remain buried and that they are healthy. If the above-ground conditions are maintained, healthy box turtles should fare well during this cooling period. Problems will occur if the temperatures regularly rise to a level that is high enough for the turtles to become active but too low for them to resume normal activity patterns such as feeding. Under these conditions, box turtles will lose weight, become stressed, and—because their immune system is inhibited at lower temperatures—be more susceptible to diseases such as respiratory infections. Keeping the soil too moist can lead to problems also.

After three months box turtles can be warmed up and placed back on a regular feeding and maintenance schedule. (This hibernation period may be as long as five months in colder areas of the country, particularly for animals kept outdoors.)

Box turtles typically go off feed in the fall. If they are kept at normal temperatures, the turtles will lose weight, suffer from stress, and possibly die. When you are raising box turtles from hatchlings, bear in mind that in captivity most members of the *carolina* complex will shut down (indicated by fasting), not the first year, but the second or third year following hatching. For this reason it becomes critical that box turtles be hibernated once they show signs of going off feed in late fall. They can be hibernated outdoors or indoors, depending on where conditions are most suitable.

If you live in a climate that it suitable for year-round outdoor maintenance of the subspecies you are keeping, you can keep your box turtles outdoors, as long as you provide an area where the ground is soft enough for the turtles to burrow deep. You can pile alfalfa hay or leaf litter to provide additional insulation. Some keepers (particularly in cold areas) also recommend piling carpet remnants over the litter or hay.

If the turtles are hibernated indoors, you should fill a large bin—such as a large trash can or a custom-build wooden box—with a slightly moist soil and keep them in a garage, basement, or other cool area of the house. Once the turtles have buried themselves, you can add a layer of alfalfa hay on top. Hibernation in the upper 50s to low 60s F (13.9 to 17.2° C) is suitable for most species. They can safely tolerate temperatures in the 40s° F (4.4 to 9.4° C), if necessary. For cooling reptiles, apartment dwellers sometimes devote an unheated room or a bathroom to that purpose. Ninety days of hibernation is adequate for most species, although eastern box turtles from the northern part of their range can be in hibernation for as long as five months.

If hibernation is handled properly, relatively little weight loss occurs during this period.

A question that sometimes arises is whether to hibernate box turtles that are underweight. This is a difficult decision because if a turtle is underweight and refuses to feed, keeping it at normal temperatures may result in its becoming thinner faster. The first step should be to determine the turtle's state of health. You can do this to some degree by using the charts on pages 71-76. In addition, you should have a veterinarian perform a fecal check for internal parasites. Ideally, an examination also should be performed by a qualified veterinarian to determine the general state of health of the turtle. Unless the turtle is seriously emaciated, as long as it appears to be healthy, it will be a good idea to cool it down in late fall or early winter. The box turtle will lose less weight this way, and when it does come out of hibernation it will probably start feeding within a week of its return to normal conditions. With thin turtles, a minimal hibernation period of less than two months is recommended.

"Pinky" a captive-hatched albino box turtle kept as a permanent display at Reptile Haven. This hatchling when first obtained had obvious symptoms of calcium deficiency, but a suitable diet corrected the condition. The upwardly flared marginals are a common syndrome in turtles whose initial calcium deficiencies are later corrected.

Breeding

Turtle breeding occurs in the spring and commonly continues into the summer following the end of hibernation. For box turtles, breeding is an extended and vigorous affair, sometimes lasting several hours. Female box turtles can store sperm from an effective breeding for several years. Collected females maintained without males have been known to lay fertile eggs for as many as four years.

Egg Laying

Typically, more than one clutch is laid during the breeding season. Box turtles dig a shallow nest three to four inches deep in which to deposit their eggs. In captivity they usually dig at the corner of an enclosure or of a section of wood. Sometimes the eggs are laid in a small depression, right under the edge of a landscape structure, such as a

Depending on their subspecies, age, and size, box turtles will lay from two to seven (usually four to five) thin-shelled eggs per clutch.

plant or a log in the vivarium. When box turtles are kept without a suitable substrate for digging, females may lay their eggs on the ground surface. Unfortunately, eggs laid in this manner are usually damaged or broken.

Once you find them, remove the eggs from the enclosure and transfer them to a small container, such as a plastic shoe box, containing moistened sphagnum moss. Bury the eggs under a thin layer of moss. The lid should be perforated with a few holes for air exchange, and the box should be covered.

Incubation

You can incubate box turtle eggs at room temperature or higher, partially depending on the sex ratios you desire in the resulting hatchlings. You should inspect the incubating container regularly to make sure that the moss remains damp. Regular light misting is also recommended to maintain a high relative air humidity. Incubation time is 75 to 90 days.

Temperature and Sex Determination

Recent research suggests that the sex of box turtles is determined by the temperature during incubation. Eggs incubated at 71° F (21.7° C) will result mostly in males. Eggs incubated at 79° F (26.1° C) will tend to result in more or less equal numbers of males and females. Above 79° F (26.1° C), more females tend to be produced. At a temperature of 88° F (31.1° C), the great majority of hatchlings will be females.

Rearing Hatchlings

Hatchling box turtles are relatively easy to raise. You should keep them in the same manner as adults but in smaller enclosures, where you can readily monitor the animals. Provide shelters of an appropriate size. Because small box turtles tend to be more aquatic than adults, it is important to have a large, shallow water container that they can readily crawl into and out of. Water depth should be no more than one-third the height of the turtle; the lids of plastic shoeboxes work well for this purpose. Hatchling box turtles also tend to be primarily carnivorous, so a variety of foods such as canned dog food and vitamin/mineral-supplemented live foods should be offered every other day. During the growth period of young box turtles, particularly during the first year, you must be careful to provide enough calcium and vitamin D_3 in their diet or small box turtles will develop rickets. This disease is characterized by soft shell, particularly the plastron, and later by other skeletal deformities.

NOTES ON ORNATE BOX TURTLES

As a rule, ornate box turtles (*Terrapene ornata*) are less adaptable and do not acclimate as well as members of the *Terrapene carolina* complex.

Many of these animals sold in the pet trade are dead within their first six months of captivity. Younger specimens generally adapt better than older animals. These turtles must be provided with shelters (such as hollowed logs) if they are to fare well. The ground medium should not be soggy but should allow for good drainage and easy digging. Mixing some sand (approximately 25 percent) into the soil will provide an adequate consistency. Although ornate box turtles inhabit areas in which daytime temperatures are high and relative air humidity may be low, they will spend most of the day in shelters, where temperature will be more moderate and relative air humidity will be comparatively high. A light sprinkling or misting with water on warm days is beneficial. Relatively high daytime temperatures (85 to 88° F or 29.4 to 31.1° C) and moderate nighttime temperatures (70 to 75° F or 21.1 to 23.9° C) are recom-

Ornate box turtle *(Terrapene ornata)*. These turtles are often difficult to establish in captivity.

mended except during the hibernation period. A large, shallow water pan should be available at all times.

Sexing

The first hind toe of males is turned inward. In some males, the iris of the eye will be reddish. Some males also will have reddish spots on their forelimbs, as compared to the yellowish spots of females. Some males will have greenish to lime-green heads.

Diet

Many ornate box turtles are initially reluctant to feed. In the wild their diet consists primarily of insects. In captivity, a variety of live foods and meats should be offered with regularity. Food should be offered in the late afternoon, because many ornate box turtles will not feed during the heat of the day.

THE AMBOINA OR MALAYSIAN BOX TURTLE

In recent years, large numbers of common Asian box turtles *Cuora amboinensis* have been imported in the United States for sale as pets. Although these turtles also have a plastral hinge like the North American *Terrapene*, they are different enough in their requirements that they deserve a special section devoted to them.

General Information

This species is generally very hardy and easily maintained, but overcrowded and filthy conditions prior to shipping can cause these imported animals to arrive infected with protozoans and, in some cases, salmonella. As with all water turtles, owners must be careful to maintain sanitary practices, including thoroughly washing hands with antibacterial soap after handling and making sure that children do not put their hands in their mouths during or following handling. This precaution is only common sense. In a well-designed vivarium, these elegant turtles can make a very attractive display.

Compared to American box turtles, which must be considered as primarily terrestrial, the common Asian box turtle (*Cuora amboinensis*) is a semiaquatic turtle that requires a relatively large, shallow water area in order to fare well.

Selection

See section titled "Selecting a Potentially Healthy Box Turtle."

Distribution

These turtles come from the Nicobar islands, Bangladesh, Assam south through Burma, Thailand, Cambodia, Vietnam, Malaya, eastern Indonesia, Sulawesi, and Amboina. They also are found in the Philippines and the Celebes.

Size

Asian box turtles may achieve a length of eight inches.

Sexing

Males have slightly concave plastra and larger, thicker tails than females.

Housing and Maintenance

Enclosure

The best type of enclosure for maintaining Asian box turtles is a large aquarium or a plastic concrete-mixing container.

Size of Enclosure

The minimum size of an enclosure for these turtles should be 30 inches long, preferably 36 to 48 inches long.

Enclosure Design

There are several ways that an enclosure can be designed for Malaysian box turtles. The vivarium you assemble will depend on the amount of money and time that you are willing to dedicate to maintaining these animals. The following are two options for design. A key consideration,which applies to any turtle that spends a significant amount of time in water, is that healthy turtles

Feeding the turtles in a separate feeding container considerably reduces the rate of fouling the water and facilitates cleaning.

eat a lot and consequently defecate a lot, usually in their water section. This means that you must devise a system for regular changing of the water and cleaning of the water section.

Basic Enclosure

Because Asian box turtles are mostly shoreline animals, you should maintain them in enclosures with shallow water.

The Asian box turtle is often kept as a water turtle. Its tank or container can have either a bare bottom or a layer of a smooth, fine-grade rounded pea gravel. Some people design large tanks with undergravel filters, over which two inches of fine-grade pea gravel are placed. Using powerheads on the undergravel filter outlets will improve filtration. With turtles, regular changing of water will still be necessary, although not quite as frequently as with an unfiltered tank.

Build a large land area in the enclosure. It could consist of something as simple as large pieces of shale or slate, stacked to create a land area with graded access, or of a custom-made plexiglas platform above the water level with a graded access to water. It is important to provide the land area, graded access, and shallow water (a water area no deeper than half the height of the turtle, grading into a deeper area equal to or slightly greater than, the height of the turtle).

Some people simply construct a land area of piled up pea gravel gradually sloping to the water section. There are many design possibilities. Obviously, the larger the enclosure, the greater the possibilities. If the vivarium is well designed, you can include large plants in it, as long as the leaves and soft portions are outside the reach of your turtles.

Some herpetoculturists maintain Asian box turtles in modified children's plastic pools or plastic concrete-mixing containers.

Heating

The land area should be lit by an incandescent bulb or spotlight in a suitable reflector-type fixture. The temperature of the area closest to the bulb should be 85° F (29.4° C). You can heat the aquarium water with a submersible aquarium heater. A water temperature of 78 to 85° F (25.6 to 29.4° C) is suitable.

Feeding

In the wild, this Asian species is thought to be primarily vegetarian, but in captivity it will eat a variety of foods. As with the American box turtle, a varied diet is recommended. This species will feed both on land and in water. There is a risk of calcium-and-vitamin deficiency if the turtle is fed only on plant matter, unless you take great care to provide a balanced vegetarian diet. Vitamin/mineral supplementation of the diet is recommended.

Breeding

Only healthy, established animals should be considered for breeding. We recommend pre-breeding conditioning, whereby you allow daytime temperatures to drop by 5° F (2.8° C) and night temperatures by 10° F (5.5° C) for up to eight weeks during the winter. Thus, daytime temperature should be set for ten to twelve hours at 75 to 80° F (23.9 to 26.7° C) and nighttime temperatures for twelve to fourteen hours at 70 to 75° F (21.1 to 23.9° C). Correspondingly reducing the photoperiod is recommended (ten hours of light and fourteen hours of darkness). The feeding schedule should be cut to once or twice a week.

In spring and early summer, females typically lay three to four clutches of two eggs each.

Breeding should occur a few weeks after the temperature cycle is returned to normal. A land area consisting of a plastic container with several inches of potting soil should be provided in which the female can lay her eggs.

Incubation

Hatchlings of Asian box turtles are 1 1/2 inches long. For more information on incubation of Asian box turtle eggs, see "Chinese Box Turtles" under "Incubation" in the following section.

Chinese Box Turtles

The Chinese box turtle has recently been imported in increasing numbers. It is relatively hardy and tends to fare well in captivity.

Scientific Name

Cuora flavomarginata

Distribution

This species comes from southern China, Taiwan, and the Ryukyu Islands.

Size

Four and one-half to seven inches

Sexing

The plastron of the male is rounded both front and back, whereas the back portion of the female's plastron bends slightly upward. The base of the tail of males is thicker than that of females.

Enclosure Design

You can keep these Chinese turtles like American box turtles, as long as you include a large shallow container of water. Such a container may be difficult to find, but large plastic trays can serve well for the purpose. A large cat-litter pan sunken in the ground will work if you design a graded access that allows the turtle to get in and out of the tray easily.

In addition to providing the water container, it is a good idea once a week to place a Chinese box turtle in a container with water no deeper than one-third its height for a few hours. This procedure will allow the turtle to soak, thus ensuring that it is getting enough water.

Temperature

The optimum temperature for Chinese box turtles is 75 to 85° F (23.9 to 29.4° C). This species is not tolerant of very cold temperatures. A minimum nighttime temperature of 70° F (21.1° C) is recommended except during winter cooling when nighttime temperatures may be allowed to drop to as low as 65° F (18.3° C).

Feeding

Although the Chinese box turtle is not as finicky as the American box turtle, it should be offered a similarly varied diet. In addition to meats, this species will also eat fish (small feeder goldfish for example). The Chinese box turtle likes to feed both on land and in shallow water.

Breeding

At this writing, not much information is available on the captive breeding of this species. You should initiate pre-breeding conditioning only with healthy and established animals. This author recommends a 5 to 10° F (2.8 to 5.5° C)

Chinese box turtle (left) next to a Malayan box turtle (right) which stubbornly refused to pose for a picture.

drop in daytime temperature and a 10° F (5.5° C) drop in nighttime temperature during the winter for two to three months. The health of the turtles should be carefully monitored during this period. These turtles should breed in the spring after the temperature range is set back to normal. The author recommends reducing the photoperiod in the winter to ten hours of daylight per day and increasing it in the spring to 14 hours of daylight per day. (See Asian box turtle.)

Incubation

The Chinese box turtle species normally breeds in the spring. Females lay several single egg clutches per year. Suitable egg incubation temperatures are 77 to 82° F (25 to 27.8° C) under conditions similar to those indicated for American box turtles. Eggs hatch in approximately two months. Hatchlings are one and three-fourths inches long and tend to be more aquatic than adults.

Source Materials

Conant, R. A. Field Guide to Reptiles and Amphibians of Eastern and Central North America. *The Peterson Field Guide Series.* Boston: Houghton Mifflin. 1975.

Ernst, C.H., and R. Barbour. Turtles of the World. Washington, D.C.: *Smithsonian Institution, Press.* 1989.

Highfield, A.C. Keeping and Breeding Tortoises. England: R & A Publishing. 1990.

Pope, C.H. Turtles of the United States and Canada. New York: Alfred A. Knopf. 1939.

Smith, M.A. "The Fauna of British India." *Reptilia and Amphibia,* Vol. I, Loricata and Testudines. London: Taylor and Francis. 1931.

Slavens, F. and K. Slavens. Reptiles and Amphibians in Captivity: Breeding, Longevity and Inventory. Seattle, Washington: Slaveware, 1992.

The Recognition and Treatment of Diseases and Disorders in Box Turtles

By Roger J. Klingenberg, D.V.M.

Box turtles are perceived by the general public as being among the hardiest and easiest of reptiles to care for. Perhaps the bright-eyed appearance of healthy box turtles busily clamoring about in its armored home causes us to view them as indestructible. Unfortunately, these perceptions have caused these animals to be among the most neglected reptiles maintained in captivity.

As with any captive reptile, you must meet many specialized husbandry techniques to insure the turtle's continued health (see de Vosjoli Part 1). The following husbandry considerations are presented with respect to their importance in maintaining the overall health of the captive box turtle.

Husbandry Considerations and Their Impact on Health Maintenance

Providing Heat

Current veterinary knowledge places great emphasis on providing turtles with a usable thermal gradient[1]. Research has demonstrated that terrestrial turtles will take advantage of a thermal gradient in their day-to-day behavior[2]. Following a feeding, turtles bask significantly more and show an increased precision of thermoregulation. When turtles are infected with bacteria they seek warmer sites, thereby creating a "fever." This behavioral fever has been shown to have survival value and is impossible to achieve without a usable thermal gradient[3]. Studies on the administration of the antibiotic Amikacin® to turtles and tortoises at various temperatures also support the concept that drugs will act more efficiently at appropriate temperatures, which also decrease the potential toxicity of the drug[4]. If an appropriate thermal gradient is provided, the turtle will alter its behavior in order to use the gradient to its benefit in the digestion of food and to stimulate its own immune system.

A three-toed box turtle with early symptoms of an overgrown upper beak.

Ambient daytime temperatures of 72 to 88° F (22.2 to 31.1° C) with a nighttime drop to no lower than 60° F (15.6° C) are most appropriate for box turtles. Turtles maintained in outdoor enclosures seem to sustain colder nighttime lows easily (down to 40° F or 4.4° C) if daytime temperature ranges are at a suitably warm range. Low daytime and nighttime ambient temperatures without other provisions for heat, invite maldigestion and immune-system depression. Box turtles can also tolerate exposure to temperatures higher than 88° F (31.1° C), but heat stress will occur if there is no provision for shade or a cooler section of the enclosure.

A simple aluminum reflector or clip-on desk lamp with a 60- to 75-watt incandescent bulb suspended twelve to eighteen inches above the floor of the cage function well as a spot basking site. An ideal setup in an appropriately large cage would provide at one end of the cage a basking light, which is left on for several hours daily (varied with the season), and an undertank heater at a different site in the

This author is convinced of the necessity of a basking light for turtles maintained indoors.

cage. The basking light allows for a quick warm-up during the day only. The undertank heater provides a more subtle heat source that can be utilized day or night. Of course, nonheated zones must be provided as well, to allow the turtle a full spectrum of choices. If the cage is only large enough for one heating source, this author recommends a basking light. A thermometer should be used to measure temperatures at various points in the cage, to make sure that the heat provided is neither excessive nor deficient.

Providing Light

Box turtles appear to have a crucial need for access to unfiltered ultraviolet (UV) light. The absorption of such light through the turtle's skin allows it to produce active vitamin D, which in turn is essential for the calcium absorption from the intestine[5]. Turtles housed outdoors have no problems with adequate UV exposure as unfiltered sunlight is the very best source; those housed indoors need to take outdoor "walks," which seems also to provide psychological benefits, as box turtles enjoy the increased activity. It is important not to force the turtle to sit in direct sunlight on a warm day for more than a few minutes at a time because overheating can result. Ideally, you should allow the turtle to wander in and out of sun and shade as it desires. Two to three short strolls each week will provide adequate UV access. If time and climate don't allow this, however, then it is important to provide UV light from a Chroma-50® (General Electric Co.), Vitalite® (Duro-test Lamps), or a Colortone 50® (Phillips Lighting Corp.) bulb[6]. It has been suggested that any of these bulbs in combination with black lights provide the most useful spectrum. These lights should be no higher than eighteen inches above the floor of the cage and should have no glass or plastic filtering the light. Bear in mind that sunlight or artificial light passed through glass loses more than over 98 percent of the UV light as a result of refraction.

Besides providing active vitamin D for adequate calcium absorption and utilization, UV light also seems to stimulate a box turtle's appetite and activity, especially when the light is coordinated with a timer to approximate seasonal changes.

Active vitamin D, because of its vital role in calcium metabolism, is essential to help prevent metabolic bone disease.

Correcting Dehydration

Many new box turtles are brought to the veterinarian in a very dehydrated state. Some of these turtles have been passed from collector to wholesaler to retailer with little regard for their hydration or nutrition. Perhaps their caretakers have reasoned that all turtles are similar to tortoises, which are thought to require little fluid. This reasoning is false.

A dehydrated turtle can be recognized by loss of skin elasticity and by retraction of the skin deep within the shell (see Figure 1). Because dehydration and starvation are commonly seen together, dehydrated turtles are usually very gaunt. In more advanced cases, the animal's eyes have a sunken appearance and the turtle may barely keep its eyes open. Most turtles will hydrate themselves naturally if given a shallow basin of tepid water in which to soak. The author recommends letting the dehydrated turtle soak for several hours at first; thereafter, these soaks should be limited to fifteen to twenty minutes, two to three times daily (see Figure 2). By limiting these soaking periods, you can maintain the water quality, as turtles tend to defecate while soaking. The author has seen box turtles double their original weight after the first soaking period. It is important to keep the water shallow, usually only three-fourths inch deep, so that the turtle can rest without having to raise its head out of the water. You should also allow a normal, acclimated box turtle to soak for five to ten minutes daily, rather than leave a water container in its cage. This method prevents excessive soaking, which can cause skin irritation; it also helps prevent the consumption of fecal-contaminated water. If you provide a shallow water dish, you must thoroughly clean it daily, if not more often.

Turtles that are too weak to soak or that seem indifferent to drinking can be hydrated by orally administering Gatorade® (The Gatorade Co., Chicago, Illinois) or Pedialite® (Ross Labs, Columbus, Ohio). These liquids offer easily absorbed fluids, electrolytes, amino acids, and sugars. The author prefers to administer the fluids with a ball-tipped feeding needle (Figure 3) that attaches to a syringe. A four- or five-inch, 18-gauge feeding needle is a very useful size. Figures 4 through 8 illustrate how to administer these fluids. When the turtle's neck is retracted into its shell, its esophagus is also retracted; thus it is important (and much easier) to pass a tube when the head is extended[5]. The fluids are administered at a rate not to exceed two to three percent of the total body weight per each 24-hour period. For example, a one-kilogram turtle weighs 1,000 grams, and thus two to three percent would be 1,000 x .02 to .03 = 20 to 30 grams (gm). This formula tells us that we should not administer more than 20 to 30 grams of fluid per 24-hours, but how do we determine how much fluid that is? Easy! Each milliliter (ml or cc) of fluid weighs one gram; so now we know not to exceed 20 to 30 milliliter of fluid. Table 1 lists some useful conversion values to aid in the conversion of milligrams to milliliters and pounds to kilograms. It is wise to give half the dose immediately, and then give the other half several hours later, so as not to overwhelm the turtle's intestinal tract. If the turtle is not responding by drinking on its own within 48 hours, it should be seen by a veterinarian. Hydration needs should be corrected prior to addressing nutritional requirements.

Weight and Volume Conversion Values

1 kilogram (kg)	= 1,000 grams (gm)
1 gram (gm)	= 100 milligrams (mg)
1 pound (lb)	= 454 grams (gm)
1 litre (l)	= 1,000 milliliters (ml)
1 milliliter (ml)	= 1 cubic centimeter (cc)
1 milliliter (ml)	= 1 gram (gm)
1 ounce (oz)	= 30 milliliters (ml) = 30 grams (gm)
1 teaspoon (tsp)	= 5 milliliters (ml)
1 tablespoon (tbsp)	= 3 teaspoons (tsp)
1 tablespoon (tbsp)	= 15 milliters (ml)

Figure 1: This box turtle is both dehydrated and underweight because of malnutrition. Note the severity of the dehydration as evidenced by the deeply recessed eyes.

Nutritional Supplementation

The quickest way to correct nutritional problems, of course, is to offer a suitable diet to the starving reptile. If the turtle is not feeding voluntarily, however, it can temporarily be force-fed using alimentary diet (a\d from Hills Prescription Diets) or a homemade mixture (recipe follows). Hills a\d is a chicken-based syringeable food available from veterinarians; it provides an ideal combination of nutrients, minerals, and electrolytes to prevent further tissue wasting[1]. Feed the a/d at a rate of 1/2 ounce (15 ml) per kilogram every seven to fourteen days as needed. In extreme cases you can force-feed the turtle twice the first week. Normal foods must be offered, and natural feedings are encouraged. Administer the force-feed mixtures with a ball-tipped feeding needle in exactly the same manner as described for the administration of fluids.

Homemade Force-Feed Mixture

1 jar puréed chicken baby food

1 jar Gatorade® or Pedialite®

one-fourth teaspoon vegetable oil

1 Tums® tablet, crushed (provides calcium)

Mix well and feed at the rate of ½ ounce (15 ml) per kilogram every seven to fourteen days as needed.

By initially supporting the turtle's physiological needs with an appropriate thermal gradient and an appropriate UV source, and by correcting dehydration and providing nutritional supplementation when needed, you can much more successfully manage the following disorders and diseases.

Figure 2: The easiest way to initially hydrate a turtle is to let it soak in a shallow container and allow it to drink. The author has seen dehydrated turtles double their body weight over several hours through nothing more than drinking.

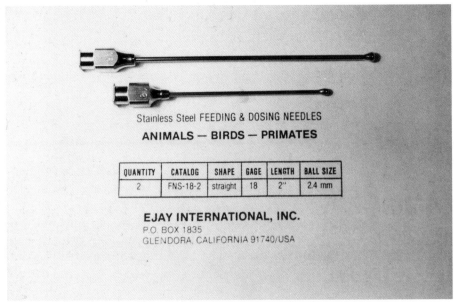

Stainless Steel FEEDING & DOSING NEEDLES
ANIMALS — BIRDS — PRIMATES

QUANTITY	CATALOG	SHAPE	GAGE	LENGTH	BALL SIZE
2	FNS-18-2	straight	18	2"	2.4 mm

EJAY INTERNATIONAL, INC.
P.O. BOX 1835
GLENDORA, CALIFORNIA 91740/USA

Figure 3: These ball-tipped feeding needles come in a variety of sizes, straight or curved. An 18-gauge catheter four to five inches long is a useful size for the average box turtle.

Figure 4: Manually extending the turtle's head help's straighten its esophagus. Grasping the turtle behind the mandibles allows its head to be extended without causing undue discomfort. Holding the turtle in a vertical position will allow gravity to aid in this process.

Figure 5: Once the head is extended, a mouth gag such as this avian mouth gag (Lafaber Co.) is introduced horizontally into the mouth and then gently rotated vertically. This is done without exerting excessive force so as not to crack the beak.

Figure 6: A plastic-coated infant spoon can be used to manipulate the mouth open and help prevent cracking of the beak. These spoons are readily available at drug and grocery stores.

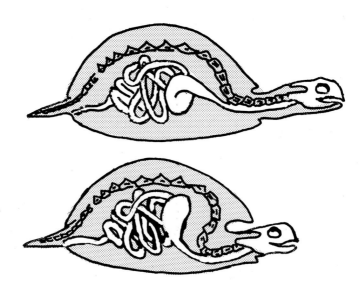

Figure 7: This drawing illustrates two important points. One is that the neck must be extended for easy passage of the feeding needle through the esophagus. Secondly, the distance necessary to pass the feeding tube is from the tip of the extended nose to the midpoint of the plastron.

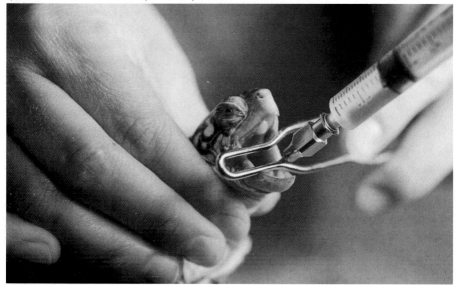

Figure 8: After the tip of the feeding needle is lubricated with water, it is guided down against the roof of the mouth and advanced to the premeasured depth. Take care to avoid the glottis at the base of the tongue. Occasionally, a mild resistance is felt as the needle passes through the esophageal sphincter. Keeping the neck extended and the turtle vertical, administer the fluids over a period of a minute. If any liquid starts to reflux (back up), immediately stop administration, remove the feeding needle, and allow the turtle to swallow. When administration is complete, keep the turtle warm and allow it to remain undisturbed for several hours.

THE VITAMIN A STORY AND ITS IMPORTANCE TO THE BOX TURTLE

There are two sources of vitamin A: beta-carotene and preformed vitamin A found in digested food. The major source is beta-carotene which, is found in the yellow pigment of plants. The greener the plant, the higher the beta-carotene content. When a plant turns brown, there is a proportional loss of beta-carotene. After carotene is ingested, it is absorbed by the intestinal mucosal cells in the gastrointestinal tract and is cleared to form two vitamin A molecules. The other source of vitamin A is from preformed vitamin A contained in food such as prey animals. Because box turtles are true opportunistic omnivores, they derive their vitamin A from both sources.

Vitamin A is a member of the family of fat-soluble vitamins: A, D, E, and K. Unlike water-soluble vitamins such as B and C, which pass out of the body when required levels are met, fat-soluble vitamins can be stored in the body, primarily in the liver. While storage of vitamins is a definite advantage, it is also a liability because toxic levels can be attained. In order for storage to occur, the vitamin A intake must be at least three times the amount required for daily maintenance, and this level must be maintained for three to six months before storage will begin[7,8]. Vitamin A requirements increase with growth, pregnancy, and stress. Regardless of its mother's vitamin A stores, a newborn animal has minimal vitamin A stored and thus is dependent on its new diet to obtain adequate amounts[9].

What does vitamin A do in the body that makes it so important? In the eye's retina, vitamin A combines with the protein opsin to form the photopigment rhodopsin. Rhodopsin is then incorporated into the outer segments of the retinal photoreceptors. Light absorbed by the photoreceptors induces cleavage of rhodopsin, stimulating electrical impulses that travel to the brain, where they are interpreted as vision. Vitamin A affects vision by three mechanisms: (a) by limiting rhodopsin formation; (b) by affecting changes in the corneal and lacrimal cells; and (c) by affecting bone development, which can lead to pinching of the optic nerve.

> Vitamin A has two distinct biological functions within the body: it helps (a) vision and (b) cell division and differentiation.

Vitamin A also serves to control the rate of cell division and to ensure each cell a specific pattern of differentiation and function. In addition to affecting the cells used for vision, vitamin A also affects cells in the reproductive tract, bone, and epithelial linings.

The main causes of vitamin A deficiency in box turtles is inadequate diet. The diets that usually precipitate these problems are: (a) commercial turtle food, (b) lettuce-based diets, (c) all-meat diets, and (d) all-fruit diets. These diets can lead to other vitamin or mineral disorders as well. Commercial turtle foods seldom contain enough vitamin A or other nutrients to serve as a sole diet, because vitamin A—in the form of carotene or preformed vitamin A—is highly unstable. Fruit has limited vitamin A content. Lettuce, although green, is a poor source of any nutrients and its vitamin A content is marginal. The solution in mild and early cases of vitamin A deficiency is to feed a well-formulated and complete diet. The section on feeding should be carefully reviewed.

Signs of vitamin A deficiencies are listed on page 82. It is important to realize that the treatment and rehabilitation of

Box Turtle Health Troubleshooting Chart—I

Anatomical Area	Symptoms	Most Common Cause	Treatment
Head			
1) Eyes	Red, swollen, bubbly	Bacterial conjunctivitis, often complicated by vitamin A deficiency, or secondary to respiratory infections	Apply small amount of a triple antibiotic opthalmic ointment to eyes 3 times daily for 7–10 days. If mild conjunctivitis, it will resolve quickly. If eyes do not respond, vitamin A deficiency should be addressed. If signs of respiratory infection, treat the underlying problem.
	White, opaque caps, unable to see eyes (see Figures 9 & 10)	Bacterial conjunctivitis with caseated pus	Apply triple antibiotic ointment to eye 3 times daily. Once eye can be easily opened, gently pry loose the pus and lift out with a cotton swab. Do not force. Continue to apply ointment for several more days.
	Sticky eyes, won't open, thick secretions	Vitamin A deficiency	Administer daily soaks to allow turtle to wash eyes. Hydrate eyes with artificial tears or opthalmic antibiotic ointment applied 3 times daily for at least 2–4 weeks. With mild cases add 1–2 drops of cod liver oil to food twice weekly. Severe cases need to see veterinarian for vitamin A injection. See expanded vitamin A notes following the chart.
2) Nostrils	Bubbles, chronic nasal discharge (see Figure 11)	Respiratory infection, often complicated by vitamin A deficiency	Increase heat to stimulate immune system. Make sure vitamin A deficiency is not a factor. If nasal discharge is clear, it may be a simple vitamin A deficiency. If discharge is colored it is likely bacterial. Both can occur together. If turtle is eating well and kept warm and dry, some of these infections are self-limiting. If not resolved within 10 days or is worsening, see veterinarian for appropriate antibiotics.

Box Turtle Health Troubleshooting Chart—II

Anatomical Area	Symptoms	Most Common Cause	Treatment
Head			
3) Mouth	Mild distortion, hemmorrhagic spots, viscous secretions, excess salivation (see Figure 12)	Infectious stomatitis (mouth rot)	Increase heat. Gently remove loose tissue and clean with Nolvasan®, Betadine®, or peroxide. In all but the mildest cases, see veterinarian for antibiotics.
	Beak overgrowth (see Figure 13)	Eating small, prepared meals with little chewing or biting required. Also seen with calcium deficiency as skull develops abnormally	In mild cases gently grind down with nail file until eating is no longer impaired. In advanced cases, see veterinarian who can trim excess tissue and grind down to appropriate shape. Avoid excessive trimming so that blood line is not hit.
4) Throat	Puffing out throat, extending neck, gaping mouth	Respiratory infection	See previous treatment listed under "nostrils" and respiratory treatment plan.
5) Cheeks	Unilateral or bilateral swelling near angle of jaw. Causes assymetry of head. Inability or reluctance to eat (see Figures 14 & 15)	Bacterial infection of the middle ear	Requires lancing over tympanic membrane and removing the trapped, caseated pus. The area must be carefully scraped to remove all infected material and then flushed with Nolvasan® or Betadine® solution and then packed with an antibiotic ointment. Area is flushed and packed daily for 7–10 days. If area is not healing well or turtle won't eat, see veterinarian for systemic antibiotics.
6) Neck & Forelegs	Lumps visible under the skin	Biting fly larvae (Botfly larvae)	See myasis discussion under skin disorders. These lumps are commonly visible on the neck and forelegs but can occur on any skin surface anywhere on the body.

Box Turtle Health Troubleshooting Chart—III

Anatomical Area	Symptoms	Most Common Cause	Treatment
Skin			
	Mild peeling of skin	Oversoaking	Remove drinking dish and limit to short soak.
	Severe peeling of skin with exposure of red, moist tissue underneath	Hypervitaminosis A (excessive vitamin A)	Peeling will usually resolve within 2–4 weeks. Keep turtle on newspaper so that a triple antibiotic ointment (Neosporin®, Polysporin®) can be applied to raw areas. See expanded section on vitamin A following this chart.
	Open wound with very small white larvae (maggots). May also appear as lumps under the skin. A small hole with a black crusty discharge over such a lump is indicative of botfly larvae. See Figs. 21–29.	Myiasis (infestation of a wound with maggots)	Protect turtles from biting flies that lay eggs at the edges of small wounds. Hatching maggots invade wound. Maggots must be plucked out with tweezers and the hole flushed with Polvasan®, Betadine®, or peroxide and all loose tissue debris cleaned away from the site. Pack an antibiotic ointment into the site daily until healed. If massively involved see veterinarian for a systemic antibiotic and to check the site. See expanded section on parasitic flies.
Shell			
	Eroded, roughened areas of shell. May be soft and discolored.	Infected shell (shell rot); usually bacteria and fungus	Gently remove any loose or peeling material. Increase heat. Apply Betadine® ointment or solution daily for 2–3 weeks. Keep turtle on newspaper and change paper often. See veterinarian if not responding well.

Box Turtle Health Troubleshooting Chart—IV

Anatomical Area	Symptoms	Most Common Cause	Treatment
Shell			
	Cracked or broken shell (see Figs. 16–18)	Trauma	If shell is stable, clean with Nolvasan® or Betadine®, then apply triple antibiotic ointment. If very unstable, apply gauze over ointment and tape in place. Contact veterinarian skilled in repairing shells with fiberglass patches or bone cement. Even the most severe fractures can be repaired if tissues are protected and the turtle is promptly seen by a veterinarian.
	Malformed, soft shell, overgrown beak	Metabolic bone disease	If shell is mildly soft, correct diet and provide UV light. If severe, see veterinarian for evaluation of calcium metabolism. Overgrown beak may be due to abnormal skull formation.
	Blood on underside, blood seen under plastron epithelial lining	Bacteremia (septicemia)	Increase heat to stimulate immune system. Generally indicates a severe infection; a veterinarian should be consulted for systemic antibiotic therapy.
Gastrointestinal			
	Loose, mucus-laden stools with or without blood present	Bacterial gastroenteritis or parasites	A fecal examination must be performed to look for parasites. See Parasite treatment section following this chart. If no parasites are found, a fecal culture may be indicated. Numerous bacteria, including Salmonella species, are implicated in these cases and a systemic antibiotic is generally indicated.

Box Turtle Health Troubleshooting Chart—V

Anatomical Area	Symptoms	Most Common Cause	Treatment
Gastrointestinal			
	Tubular mass protruding from cloaca	Prolapsed organ: cloacal tissue, intestine, urinary bladder, penis, or uterus	Organ must be carefully identified. Keep moist (wrap gently in moist gauze) and call veterinarian immediately. Organ may need to be gently cleaned and dehydrated, and replacement attempted. If tissue dries excessively or becomes infected, survival rate drops quickly.
Reproductive Tract			
	Male turtle with large red-purple mass hanging from cloacal area (see Fig. 19)	Prolapsed penis	Male turtle may be sexually stimulated, and simple handling may cause reduction of penis. If prolapse is noticed early and tissue is not dried out, gently lubricate with Vaseline®, Neosporin®, or similar lubricant, and gently replace by pushing into cloaca with a cotton swab. Do not force! If in doubt or if problem persists, call veterinarian.
	Female turtle with legs thrust backward, with history of restlessness and digging	Egg bound	Rehydrate if female turtle is weak and dehydrated. Create an appropriate egg-laying site (see Breeding section). If eggs are not passed within hours of being placed in warm, quiet area with egg-laying media, see veterinarian for potential oxytocin and calcium treatment. Look for concurrent signs of vitamin A deficiency.

Box Turtle Health Troubleshooting Chart—VI

Anatomical Area	Symptoms	Most Common Cause	Treatment
Limbs			
	Overgorwn nails (see Fig. 20)	Lack of normal digging and wear in captivity	Extend limb so that nails are easily visible. Clip excess nail tips without coming within 1/8 inch of the pink blood line. If accidentally nicked, stop bleeding either by applying firm pressure for two minutes or by applying a coagulant like silver nitrate or KwikStop®.
	Swollen feet or forelimbs	Abscesses. ce;j;otos. trauma	If an abscess or a cellulitis (spreading infection) is suspected, then a veterinarian should be seen to create drainage, if necessary, and initiate antibiotics. Swelling due to trauma will usually improve without treatment.
	Rotted, eroded, or distorted toes	Fungus, occasionally caused by burns	Increase heat. Place turtle on newspaper substrate to keep clean. Gently clean and remove any loose tissue. Apply Betadine® ointment or solution daily for 2–3 weeks. If turtle does not respond to treatment, see veterinarian
General appearance			
	Declining appetite in the fall, sluggish movement, appears to be depressed	Hibernation-induced anorexia	If turtle is in good health, prepare it for hibernation (see section on Hibernation). If turtle is not well, then it must be evaluated and all problems resolved. If impossible to hibernate, then good thermal gradient and light must be utilized to attempt to stimulate the turtle to eat and drink through the winter.

turtles with severe hypovitaminosis A (vitamin A deficiency) are neither fast nor easy. A minimum of two weeks is required, and in many cases it takes several weeks. The goals for treatment of hypovitaminosis A are: (a) correction of the vitamin A deficiency, (b) opening and correcting eye lesions, (c) control of secondary eye and respiratory infections, and (d) supportive care.

All-meat diets, with the exception of fish and liver, also lack adequate vitamin A.

In milder cases, one to two drops of cod liver oil may be added to the food twice weekly for several weeks[7]. This regimen has also been advocated for healthy turtles prior to hibernation, in order to provide adequate levels of vitamin A[10]. The new vitamins for reptiles, such as Herptivite® (Rep-Cal Labs, Los Gatos, CA), used twice a week on food, could also be helpful. Hypervitaminosis from oral sources appears to be quite rare in box turtles[5]. In severe cases, an injection of vitamin A at levels of 500 to 2,000 IU per kilogram of body weight IM (intramuscularly), given once and repeated in two weeks, appears to be a safe level. The author uses Aquasol A Parenteral (Armour Pharmaceuti-

Figure 9: This turtle has an opaque layer of caseated pus trapped over its cornea and within its eyelids. The pus originated from a bacterial infection, which was secondary to an underlying vitamin A deficiency.

Figure 10: After it was hydrated by daily soaks and topical antibiotic ointments, this caseated pus literally popped out of the eyelids when gently manipulated with a cotton swab. The remainder was gently removed, and ointment was continued for several more days.

cal Co., Kankakee, IL). Levels more than 5,000 IU per kilogram of body weight weekly for two to four weeks induced severe sloughing of skin[11].

The eyes of vitamin A deficient box turtles are sealed shut, primarily because the effects of the deficiency on the lining cells of the corneal and lacrimal systems. Although the eyes appear to be excessively moist from the thick secretions and stickiness, quite the opposite is true. The eyes are so dry and void of lacrimal secretions that replenishing and maintaining their moisture is crucial. We recommend that you give each turtle a tepid 15- to 30-minute water bath once or twice daily. This bath allows the turtle to rub loose some of the dried secretions, both from the eye and from any respiratory system involvement. Following the bath, apply an ophthalmic antibiotic eye ointment, in order to provide lubrication and moisture, and also to treat any secondary bacterial infections. Eye ointments should be continued until the turtle can easily open its eyes. Eye care is demanding and slow, but absolutely essential because a turtle won't eat unless its eyes are comfortable and functional.

Secondary bacterial infections of the respiratory tract commonly accompany vitamin A deficiency. Pathogenic bacteria simply take advantage of a weakened host, which is likely to have a damaged epithelial lining because vitamin A is necessary for maintaining this lining of the respiratory tree. Note that a nasal discharge does not necessarily mean an infection exists. A serous (clear mucous) discharge common to vitamin A deficiencies because of cellular abnormalities of the nasal mucosal lining. Bacterial infections should be suspected if the nasal discharge is not clear. A gram stain or culture may be required to determine the significance of a nasal discharge.

And finally, box turtles are born with minimal vitamin A stores. Their daily requirements and eventual storage are met only when they eat an adequate and proper diet. Stress

Figure 11: This turtle demonstrates a bubbling from the nostrils. A clear nasal discharge in a turtle that is eating and feeling well is likely caused by a vitamin A deficiency. If the nasal discharge becomes colored, is excessively heavy, or is accompanied by breathing difficulties, then a respiratory infection is present.

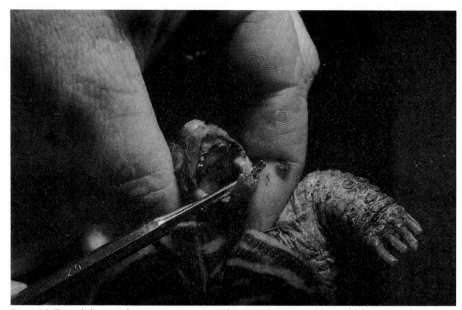

Figure 12: This turtle has an infectious stomatitis, or mouth rot. It is characterized by a mild distortion and positioning of the mouth and the accumulation of infected debris in the mouth.

It is often difficult to determine the presence of a vitamin A deficiency.

in the form of poor husbandry practices will further deplete vitamin A stores, rapidly leading to a number of health problems. As cell differentiation is one of the most important functions of vitamin A, most organ systems are affected when there is a deficiency. While signs relating to the eye and respiratory system are the most common, the reproductive, skeletal, and urinary systems—as well as the gastrointestinal tract—can be affected adversely. For instance, not all turtles with vitamin A deficiency show respiratory problems. Conversely, respiratory infections need not have an underlying vitamin A deficiency. Perhaps the best way to diagnose a vitamin A deficiency is if the turtle has a history of being maintained on a diet lacking in vitamin A, and at the same time exhibits several of the signs previously discussed. Treatment is important but should proceed conservatively, in order to prevent vitamin A toxicity. Remember: vitamin A toxicity is rarely induced orally when it is administered prudently.

Figure 13: This turtle's beak has overgrown because of a lack of normal biting and chewing activities in captivity. Less commonly, this will be a chronic problem in a turtle suffering from low calcium levels and whose skull formed in such a manner that its beak does not wear down well.

Figure 14: This box turtle has a middle-ear infection, which causes it to have an asymmetrical swelling over the cheek area. The swelling results from a build-up of caseated pus, which pushes on the tympanic membrane.

Signs of Vitamin A Deficiency

Eyes

1. Swollen lids, often stuck shut

2. Photophobia (light sensitivity)

3. Corneal opacity

4. Initial discharge, which then thickens and dries.

5. Blindness

6. Birth of eyeless or blind offspring

Gastrointestinal Effects

1. Anorexia, weight loss

2. Diarrhea

Reproductive Effects

1. Abortion

2. Sterility

3. Birth defects

Respiratory Effects

1. Increased susceptibility to pneumonia

2. Nasal discharge

3. Wheezing and sneezing

4. Open-mouth breathing

Skeletal Effects

1. Bony abnormalities

Skin

1. Excessive keratin layers, especially on head skin, cornea, and mucous membranes

Figure 15: Middle-ear infections are treated by lancing and removing the adherent pus from the middle ear. This photograph illustrates the solid nature of the caseated pus removed from such an abscess.

Figure 16: Hit by a car, this turtle has multiple shell fractures and is very unstable. Its open wounds can be gently cleaned with Betadine® or Nolvasan® solution and then lightly coated with a triple antibiotic ointment.

Figure 17: After the major wounds have been cleaned and medicated, gauze is placed over them and a bandage of medical tape is applied. This procedure will stabilize the turtle until it can be taken to a veterinarian.

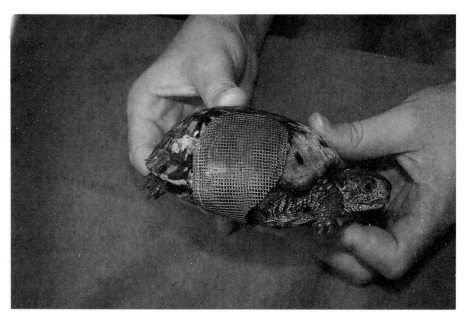

Figure 18: Shell fractures can be repaired by using fiberglass screen and epoxy glue or bone cement. In this picture, the first of three layers of fiberglass screen is being glued in place.

Figure 19: A prolapsed penis in a turtle.

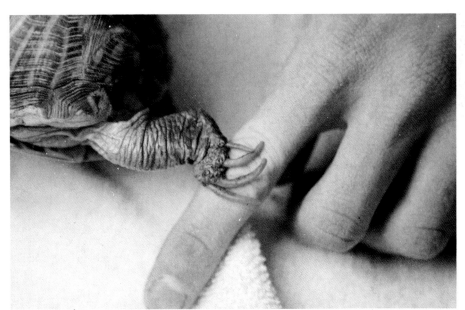

Figure 20: This turtle has overgrown nails caused by a lack of normal activity and digging in its captive environment. It is important to trim the nails to prevent them from breaking.

Treating Parasites in Box Turtles

Protozoan parasite infestations, including amebiasis, are common in turtles. These parasites can be treated with metronidazole (Flagyl) at a dosage of 25 to 40 milligrams per kilogram of body weight, given orally, mixed with food, or tubed. This dose should be given on days one and three, and repeated only if necessary[12].

Nematode parasites are perhaps the most common of the endoparasites (internal parasites). These are treated with Fenbendazole (Panacur) at a dosage of 25 milligrams per kilogram of body weight, given orally, mixed with food, or tubed. This dose should be repeated at least three times at two-week intervals[12].

Cestodes (tapeworms) can be treated with Praziquantel (Droncit) at a dose of five to eight milligrams per kilogram of body weight, given orally or by intramuscular (IM) injection. This dosage should be repeated in two weeks[12].

Ivermectin (Ivomec) is not meant for turtles and should not be given to your box turtle under any circumstances. This drug can cross the blood/brain barrier and cause paresis (partial paralysis), paralysis, or even death[12].

Remove ticks by gently but firmly pulling them out and cleaning the wound with Nolvasan®, Betadine®, or peroxide. If a swollen area larger than a pea develops at the site of the tick bite, an abscess may be forming; it may require opening, cleaning, and treating with antibiotics.

PARASITIC FLIES IN BOX TURTLES

In many regions of the United States, several species of parasitic flies lay their eggs on box turtles at the site of any type of open wound, even small abrasions and scratches. In warm weather these eggs can hatch in less than a day, and the resulting larvae or maggots invade the wound and feed on the tissue of the host. This invasion of a wound by

Figure 21: This box turtle had extensive wounds created by parasitic bites. Parasitic flies often lay eggs at the margins of and within such wounds, leading to an invasion of larvae referred to as myiasis.

Figure 22: A close-up of the turtle in Figure 21 reveals the presence of small white maggots within the wound.

maggots is referred to as myiasis and represents one step in the life cycle of the flies. This problem can be very simple or it can become so severe as to kill the host.

While they are feeding, the maggots continue to grow and develop; within 20 to 50 days they eventually drop off the turtle to pupate (the next stage in their lifecycle). Contrary to popular belief, maggots do not feed on healthy, viable tissue but rather on dead tissue and secretions associated with injured tissue. The mechanical irritation and movement of the maggots, however, serves to spread infections and to further injure tissue, thereby creating more feeding opportunities.

A successful parasite tries to coexist with its host(s), as the destruction of a host also eliminates the parasite eventually. Many wild-caught box turtles exhibit nodular scars on their necks or limbs, where maggots previously grew and developed. These turtles survive because of normal healing processes after the maggots have left the host. Fatal reactions can occur, generally as a result of secondary bacterial infections in the injured tissue.

Figure 23: The lump on the side of this turtle's neck is a pocket produced by the invasion of botfly larvae. Unlike the example in Figures 21 and 22, these flies do not require the presence of a wound to deposit their larvae; they often create their own wound by biting the turtle. Note the black spot in the center of the lump, which is the opening crusted over with dried blood and tissue debris.

Figure 24: By extending the box turtle's leg, we can see another lump just in front of the leg. This lump doesn't readily show an opening, but one is visible when the leg is moved and examined.

Figure 25: Another botfly lump is present on this turtle's rump. Although they are more common around the neck and forelegs, pockets of these parasitic flies can occur anywhere on the turtle's body.

Figure 26: After lancing this lump at the site of the opening, maggots can be seen extruding from the opening. The maggots are picked out with fine tweezers, after which the pocket is thoroughly flushed, then packed with an antibiotic ointment.

Figure 27: Fifty-nine maggots were extracted from nearly a dozen lumps on one box turtle.

Myiasis tends to occur in one of two forms. Many flies lay their eggs at the site of an existing wound and the resulting maggots hatch and feed on the surface tissue (see Figures 21 and 22). In this form of myiasis, the maggots must be rinsed or plucked off, and the wound must be cleaned thoroughly with Nolvasan®, Betadine®, or peroxide. A topical antibiotic ointment (Neosporin®, Polysporin®) should then be applied, and the wound cleaned and treated on a daily basis. In severe cases, a veterinarian should be consulted to evaluate the extent of the tissue damage and to prescribe a systemic antibiotic if necessary.

The second and more severe form of myiasis is caused by a group of parasitic flies often referred to as Botflies. In box turtles a common parasite is the "flesh fly," *Sarcophaga cistudinis.* These flies do not need a preexisting wound; they lay their eggs near a small wound or abrasion, or actually create enough of a wound with their own bite[14]. Once hatched, the larvae burrow beneath the skin and form

Figure 28: This turtle was hit by a car and sustained severe damage to its shell and underlying tissue.

Figure 29: Upon closer inspection, pastel-colored egg masses were observed in some of the injured tissue in the turtle shown in Figure 28. These eggs masses must be thoroughly cleaned off to prevent their hatching, which in warm weather can occur within 24 hours.

pockets, usually in the axillary or inguinal region, limbs, or neck. These appear as lumpy masses and, when observed closely, reveal an opening (see Figures 23–25). This opening may be almost completely closed and is usually accompanied by dried blood and secretions, creating a crusty appearance at the rim of the opening.

Treatment is initiated by making a small surgical slit with a sterile scapel in the area of the opening if it is not large enough to enter with a forceps or fine tweezers. The larvae may leave the pocket when flushed with peroxide, but usually they must be forcibly removed with tweezers (see Figure 26). Although most turtles will have only a few botfly larvae, the turtle pictured in Figure 26 had 59 botfly larvae removed (Figure 27). One of the lumpy masses on this same turtle contained twelve botfly larvae, and two others had nine each. Once the larvae are removed, the pocket should be vigorously flushed with Nolvasan®, Betadine®, or peroxide. An antibiotic ointment should then be packed into these pockets every 48 hours until the lesions are no longer draining and begin to heal with a normal-looking scab. Extensive cases will require the services of a veterinarian to remove the larvae, evaluate the tissue damage, initiate antibiotics, and provide supportive care.

Injured and/or affected turtles must be protected from flies. A good method is to place these turtles in an enclosure with cheesecloth or screen stretched over the openings. The eggs of these flies are easily visible; they are pastel-colored clumps, which you should remove whenever you observe them (see Figures 28 and 29).

HIBERNATION AND THE BOX TURTLE

Hibernation, the regular cycle of dormancy, is important for three reasons: (a) hibernation helps turtles achieve their life expectancies, (b) it helps maintain normal hormonal activity (especially of the thyroid gland), and (c) it helps stimulate and synchronize their reproductive cycles[10]. In the wild, when the turtles emerge from hibernation in the spring, the males are interested in breeding, and ovulation occurs in females at a predictable time. It is easy to understand why the species as a whole needs to hibernate in order to continue reproduction, but what about the individual turtles kept in captivity? Is hibernation essential to them as well?

Hibernation is not only desirable; it is essential for the long-term maintenance of box turtles.

As a veterinarian who specializes in reptiles, this author has owned and observed literally hundreds of box turtles through the years. The typical box turtle starts to become sluggish and lose its appetite in the early fall, September through October, and often tries to burrow and hide, whereas it had been active before. This urge to hibernate is not caused only by temperature and lighting alterations; it is a hormonally stimulated event. Even if you maintain perfect husbandry conditions, the turtle's instinct is to hibernate. Turtles that are denied the opportunity to hibernate and held in their normal cage will simply brumate. In the state of brumation, a turtle is not cool enough to hibernate but isn't fully active metabolically either. Brumating turtles generally lose as much as ten to fifteen percent of their body weight, as well as critical stores of nutrients such as vitamin A. Cells important to the immune system (especially lymphocytes) are reduced in number during the winter months[13], so that the turtle becomes both nutritionally and immune-compromised, and health problems usually ensue.

Some box turtles fare well over one winter and make up for any weight and nutrient imbalances by becoming more active in the spring; however, the effects of not hibernating over more than one winter will eventually catch up with a turtle, its health will decline, and its life expectancy will plummet.

For a discussion on how to hibernate the box turtle, see the section on hibernation.

The following points concerning hibernation are also important to bear in mind.

1. Stop feeding your turtle at least ten days prior to initiating hibernation. If the food in the upper intestinal system is not allowed to be processed it will simply "rot" there, possbily leading to infection and toxicity. Most turtles stop eating on their own. Animals maintained outside with exposure to grass and other high fiber-content foods tend to stop feeding on their own prior to hibernation. A small content of fibrous material does not appear to cause problems[10].

2. Nutrients become depleted during hibernation, especially vitamin A. Give 1 to 2 drops of cod liver oil or use a high quality multivitamin such as Herptivite® twice a week for a month prior to hibernation[10].

3. Never allow an animal that is dehydrated, suffering from poor nutrition, or ill to enter hibernation. Turtles with infections prior to hibernation must be supported with good husbandry techniques and treated with appropriate medications. Provide any necessary hydration and nutrition support as previously discussed. Once the infection or other health concerns have been addressed, the turtle should be allowed to hibernate for a short time, four to six weeks.

4. It has been this author's experience that box turtles dehydrate very easily during hibernation. To combat dehydra-

tion, this author hibernates box turtles in plastic sweater-storage boxes that have four to five inches of lightly moistened substrate consisting of newspaper strips and peat moss. The substrate should be kept damp, but not wet. If you can produce moisture by squeezing a handful of the mixture, it is too wet. The sweater boxes have several small holes for air passage, yet not enough to allow the contents to dry.

Once every two to three weeks, the substrate should be checked to see if it is moist enough. At this time, allow the turtle to soak in a shallow container for one to two hours before placing it back into its container. This is also a good time to examine the turtle for symptoms such as eyes that won't open, difficulty breathing, bubbling from nostrils, and so on. If you see any ailments, remove the turtle from hibernation, place it in normal husbandry conditions again, and take steps to remedy all problems. Turtles that are doing well can easily be hibernated for three to four months.

5. In hibernating hundreds of turtles over the years, this author has found that if the average turtle is allowed to soak and drink every three weeks, it will typically lose only one to three percent of its body weight. If a turtle has lost more than five to seven percent of its body weight and does not regain this weight after hydration, then you should remove the turtle from hibernation and have it evaluated.

Hibernating Tropical Box Turtles

Tropical box turtles, or those from the southeastern United States do not require as intense a hibernation period as do other box turtles. Those from the Southeast will thrive after being hibernated for a short period, only four to six weeks. Tropical turtles usually undergo a period of inactivity associated with the dry season in the areas from which they originate. This period of rest likely has an important influence on their hormonal metabolism, so it is advisable to try to duplicate this situation[10]. To simulate this period, simply reduce light intensity and diminish feedings. Temperatures need not be reduced except through shorter exposure to a basking light. This period should last for about six weeks.

Reference Sources

[1] Klingenberg, R.J. "Reptile Therapeutics." *In Reptile Medicine and Surgery.* 1st Edition, Mader, D.R., (ed). WB Saunders Publishing Co. (At press.)

[2] Gatten, R.E. "Aspects of the Environmental Physiology of Amphibians and Reptiles." *Proceedings of AAZV,* Greensboro, North Carolina, 1989.

[3] Mader, D.R. "The Interrelationship Between Ambient Temperature and Reptile Health Management." *Proceedings of the Second Annual Symposium on Captive Propagation and Husbandry of Reptiles and Amphibians,* Northern California Herpetological Society. 1985. Special Publication No. 3, pp. 39–48.

[4] Caligiuri, R., Kollias, G.V., Jacobsen, E.R. et al. "The Effects of Ambient Temperature on Amikacin Pharmacokinetics in Gopher Tortoises." *J. Vet. Pharm. The.* 1990. 13: 287–291.

[5] Boyer, T.H. "Common Problems of Box Turtles." *The Bulletin of the Association of Reptilian and Amphibian Veterinarians.* 1992; 2(1): 9–14.

[6] Boyer, T.H. "Box Turtle Care in Captivity." *The Bulletin of the Association of Reptilian and Amphibian Veterinarians.* 1992; 2(1): 14–16.

[7] Klingenberg, R.J. "Vitamin A Deficiency in Turtles." *Journal of the NOAH,* 1987. 13(2): 25–34.

[8] Frye, F.L. "The Role of Nutrition in the Successful Management of Captive Reptiles." *Proc. of the Calif. Med. Assoc. 86th Meeting and Scientific Seminar.* 1974: 5–20.

[9] Frye, F.L. Biomedical and Surgical Aspects of Captive Reptile Husbandry. Edwardsville, KS, Vet. Med. Publishing Co. 1981.

[10] Jarchow, J. "Hibernating Your Turtle Safely." Reprinted from *The Carapace,* Dec. 1989/ Jan. 1990 via notes from NOAH, 20 (11): 8–11.

[11] Boyer, T.H. "Vitamin A Toxicity." *The Bulletin of the*

Association of Reptilian and Amphibian Veterinarians. 1991; 1(1): p. 2.

[12] Klingenberg, R.J. "Treating Reptilian Parasites." *In Understanding Reptile Parasites.* Lakeside, California, Advanced Vivarium Systems, Inc. 1993.

[13] Wright, R.K., and Cooper, E.L. "Temperature Effects on Ectotherm Immune Responses." *Dev. Comp. Immunol.* (5 suppl.) 1981; 1:117–122.

[14] Murphy, J.B., and Collins, J.T. A Review of the Diseases and Treatments of Captive Turtles. Lawrence, Kansas, AMS Publishing. 1983; p. 21.

Index

Acclimation 15, 16

Breeding 5, 15, 41, 44, 52, 54, 56, 97
Buying 5

Coahuila box turtle 8
Cooling/Hibernation 41

Dehydration 62, 65, 98
Desert box turtle 8
Diet 9, 25, 26, 27, 28, 29, 30, 46, 48, 52, 54, 64, 70, 79, 80
Diseases 4, 14, 15, 42, 57, 65, 101
    See also Trouble Shooting Chart 71-76
Disorders 4, 14, 15, 57, 65, 70

Eastern box turtle 1, 7, 8, 9, 10, 12, 43
Egg Laying 44

Feeding 25, 26, 27, 29, 39, 42, 43, 52, 54, 59, 63, 64, 70, 90, 98, 99
Florida box turtle 8, 12
Force-Feed Mixture 64, 65

Gulf Coast box turtle 7, 8, 9

Handling 39, 49
Hatchlings 9, 25, 29, 42, 45, 52, 55
Heating 18, 21, 25, 41, 43, 48, 51, 52, 60, 61
Hibernating Tropical Box Turtles 99
Hibernation 41, 42, 43, 44, 48, 77, 97, 98, 99
Housing 17, 50
Humidity 17, 18, 20, 21, 22, 42, 45, 47
Husbandry 57, 59, 80, 97, 98, 99, 100

Incubation 45, 52, 55

Klauber's box turtle 8

Landscaping 21
Lighting 22, 61, 97
Longevity 12

Mexican box turtle 8

Nayarit box turtle 8

Nutritional Supplementation 64, 65

Ornate Box Turtle 7, 8, 9, 10, 12, 17, 28, 47, 48
Outdoor enclosures 17, 18, 19, 22, 60

Parasites 15, 16, 43, 87, 101
Parasitic Flies 89, 93

Selecting 13, 49
Sex 9, 15, 10, 41, 45, 48, 50, 53
Sexing 10, 48, 50, 53

Temperature 9, 17, 41-43, 45, 47, 51-52, 54, 55, 59, 60-61, 97, 99-101

Terrapene carolina bauri 8, 12
    See also Florida box turtle

Terrapene carolina carolina 7, 8
    See also Eastern box turtle.
Terrapene carolina major 7, 8
    See also Gulf Coast box turtle
Terrapene carolina mexicana 8
    See also Mexican box turtle
Terrapene carolina triunguis 7, 8
    See also Three-toed box turtle
Terrapene carolina yucatana 8
    See also Yucatan box turtle
Terrapene coahuila 8
    See also Coahuila box turtle
Terrapene nelsoni klauberi 8
    See also Klauber's box turtle
Terrapene nelsoni nelsoni 8
    See also Nayarit box turtle
Terrapene ornata ornata 7, 8, 10, 12.
    See also Ornate box turtle
Terrapene ornata luteola 8
    See also Desert box turtle
Three-toed box turtle 7, 8, 9, 10, 12

Vitamin A 69, 70, 77, 78, 79, 82, 98, 100

Vitamin A Deficiency 70, 77, 79, 80, 82, 100
Vitamin/Mineral Supplementation 29

Yucatan box turtle 8